Messages From Successful Entrepreneurs

Lessons From Highly Successful Founders, CEOs, and Senior Executives That Changed Their Industries Forever

Steven Imke

Produced in the United States of America

First Printing, 2016

ISBN-13: 978-1534700154
ISBN-10: 1534700153

KSI Enterprises
395 Scrub Oak Circle
Monument CO 80132

www.SteveBizBlog.com

About the Author

Steve's first foray into the world of small business came when he was an Invisible Fencing dealer. He operated this business on a part-time basis while remaining employed by a Fortune 500 company called Digital Equipment Corporation (DEC). While the Invisible Fencing business was not very successful for Steve, it was a valuable opportunity for him to learn important lessons about business in a relatively low-risk environment.

After ending his relationship with Invisible Fencing, he worked on a business plan for a new business idea and waited for the right opportunity to present itself. In 1994, DEC fell on hard times. Instead of bemoaning this turbulent economic tide, Steve capitalized on this opportunity. He quit his day job at DEC to found Horizon Interactive, a documentation and training company. In fact, Horizon Interactive became a vendor for DEC.

Over the next few years, Steve and his partners executed the business plan. The business grew to over $3 million in annual sales and opened offices in several states. Horizon Interactive's success drew the attention of Interleaf, a publicly held company out of Massachusetts. In 1999, Interleaf acquired Horizon Interactive.

As part of the acquisition, Steve was offered the position of VP of Operations for their services division. Under his leadership, Interleaf acquired two more businesses like

Horizon Interactive. The company grew the services side of the business from a combined $8 million in revenue to over $32 million in sales during the next two years.

In 2001, Interleaf was acquired by Broadvision, a California company during the height of the dot com era. Broadvision primarily acquired Interleaf for their XML engineers who worked on the product side of the business. Needing to divest himself from the services business, Steve and a former business partner acquired the assets of Interleaf's service business and started IC Interactive. They operated the business for a few more years until they sold it in 2003.

Being a serial entrepreneur, Steve has started and still operates three different businesses. One of his businesses is focused on real estate. The second one is focused on oil and gas. His third business is a company designed to help high net-worth investors understand the ins and outs of investing in oil and gas direct participation programs.

Steve has volunteered his time since 2003 as a mentor for SCORE, a local organization dedicated to helping entrepreneurs. He has acted as their Chapter Chairman for several years. He is also an advisory board member of his local Small Business Development Center (SBDC). In additions to his advisory role, he also acts as a counselor for the SBDC since 2003. In 2012, Steve acted as the interim director of SBDC while they conducted a national search for a permanent director. Currently, Steve is the Entrepreneurship Director at Pikes Peak Community College and writes a daily blog about small businesses.

Steve is a flaming dyslexic, which has its good points and bad points. Growing up, he remembers undergoing a board of education evaluation. When asked to draw a tree, Steve drew a series of concentric rings. When asked about his drawing, he said the rings were what you see when you cut down the tree and look at the stump. These rings tell the entire life story of the tree. The evaluator told his parents he was not normal. He should be more like the other kids and draw the tree from the side view.

However, rather than conform to the crowd, Steve embraced his out-of-the-box thinking as an asset. The upside of being dyslexic is exceptional spatial awareness and problems solving skills. Dyslexics develop these heightened skills since they are forced from an early age to compensate for things they do not do well.

Being a dyslexic in school prevented Steve from becoming a good reader. Even today, spelling and grammar are not his strong suits. Academically, Steve struggled in traditional schools. When he graduated from high school, he knew that a traditional classroom education was not for him so he joined the United States Coast Guard to learn a trade. Graduating near the top of his class in tech school, Steve realized that he learned by doing.

Steve tends to be an overly logical person. He likes to explore, document, and measure nearly every aspect of a project to find out what works and what does not. He has a propensity to focus on understanding why things are the way they are rather than how to duplicate what others have already done. Once Steve obtains a reasonable level of mastery in a specific subject area, he internalizes the knowledge and moves on to his next area of interest.

Everything of substance Steve knows about small business initially began by him reading books, listening to audiobooks, or watching others. He internalizes the salient points, then rolls up his sleeves and puts them into practice in his own business. Once Steve perfects a lesson, he makes it a point to document it and then share it with others. He calls these "Sea Stories," leveraging his old Coast Guard days. In addition to sharing his knowledge, this practice serves to further solidify his learning in his own mind while continuing to grow his knowledge base. In this way, Steve has codified over more than a decade's worth of his small business knowledge in the various books he has written.

This process has served Steve pretty well. By the time he was 42 years old, Steve had reached the point where he no longer needed to work for money. Passing this income milestone has not only allowed him the luxury to spend even more time to ponder and digest life's lessons, but also the freedom to tell it like it is without the fear of losing his job. He proudly wears jeans nearly every day. He also sports facial hair to remind himself and others that being a nonconformist and not subscribing to traditional viewpoints has its merits for entrepreneurs.

Steve constantly reads and listens to non-fiction audiobooks about politics or business related topics. He consumes current events from a huge basket of news sources every day so he can relate their messages in new and innovative ways. After internalizing a message and testing new theories, he shares his new-found wisdom with people willing to listen.

Since 2003, Steve has mentored and counseled thousands of fledgling entrepreneurs through his volunteer efforts with SCORE and SBDC. He has volunteered his expertise to help organizations like ARC, a program which helps individuals with developmental disabilities.

As cliché as it may sound, Steve is at the point in his life where it is all about using his skills and knowledge to help others to succeed. Steve never expects anything in return, but simply enjoys the appreciation he receives from the people he has helped and lives vicariously through their success. For Steve, sharing his knowledge is akin to the feeling a billionaire might have handing out $100 bills to random strangers on the street. He knows that by sharing some of the wisdom he has accumulated with clients, he can often make a positive difference in their lives. Steve is not particularly religious so helping entrepreneurs is his way of giving back and making a significant impact on the world around him.

Table of Contents

Chapter 1: The Founders & Executives

Founders and transformation executives have the ability to spot new market opportunities and the power to act upon them. Most of the time their business success was the result of several pivots along the way. This chapter follow the journey of many influential founders and executives that based on their leadership experienced hockey stick growth curves.

Think Like a Singer Sewing Machine

Issac Singer – Singer Corporation

Isaac Singer didn't invent the sewing machine. He perfected it and understood marketing. By the mid-1800 there were lots of sewing machines on the market that mimicked the actions of human hands. They took a thread on a needle and feed it down through the fabric and back up, pulling the thread tight to complete a stitch.

Sewing machines of that era were hard to maintain and often broke the thread, making them very unreliable. Singer thought outside of the box. Rather than imitate the human process of sewing he used the concept of a lock-stitch, which involved two threads: one in the top of the fabric and the other below.

Then Singer offered people the option to buy the machine on credit using an installment plan. This made owning a sewing machine within the reach of millions of Americans expanding into the western territories, and in the process created a whole new cottage industry built around the sewing machine.

When sales looked like they were reaching an apex Singer offered a trade-in program. Rather than refurbish the old machines as his competitors did, he thought outside the box again. Singer destroyed the old machines to remove any secondary market for his products, forcing people to only buy new machines.

The Singer story is a model for all small businesses.

How can you think outside the box to reinvent your industry?

The Face Of An Industry

Fred Bear – Bear Archery

Fred Bear is known as one of the pioneers of the modern archery industry. Fred was an avid bow hunter and popular writer for various outdoor and hunting magazines, as well as a film producer.

As a kid growing up I could not wait to read about his hunting exploits in Outdoor Life, and watched shows like American Sportsman to catch his latest hunt on TV. Fred would travel the world hunting exotic animals which he shared in articles and on TV shows.

As the founder of Bear Archery he built a brand identity and a business around his bow hunting passion with him as its spokesman. The way Fred built his business and brand is a model new entrepreneurs would be advised to learn more about and emulate.

However, what I would really like to highlight is how he took this industry to a whole new level. Hunting season prior to 1936 was just that: a hunting season. No consideration was given to the method used to hunt game.

Since hunting game animals with archery tackle is imminently harder than using a gun, the sport of archery was relegated to a backyard pastime and used as a legitimate hunting method by only a few dedicated enthusiasts.

Fred, being an expert marksman, gained much notoriety in archery exhibitions. He used his fame to petition the state of Michigan to create a separate archery season separate from the gun season, which they ultimately adopted.

Hunters realized that their in-state hunting opportunities could be doubled by taking up archery. Soon, other states followed the Michigan example and created separate archery-only seasons.

The sport of bow hunting experienced meteoric grown with Fred Bear and Bear Archery as its standard bearer.

Sometimes you have to examine the limitations of your industry and put together a plan to knock down barriers to achieve true and lasting success.

Are there barriers that are preventing your business and industry from reaching the next level?

What can you do to remove those barriers?

Follow A Different Path

Sam Walton - Walmart

My middle son lived in Bentonville, Arkansas: for two years which is the headquarters of Walmart. This fact made me want to learn more about Sam Walton, Walmart's founder. As with many biographical stories, Sam Walton's life provides several lessons for the entrepreneur.

Sam Walton began his career in retail when he bought into a 5&10 franchise known as Ben Franklin. He learned the retail business there, and in fact operated one of the most successful stores in the Ben Franklin chain. When it came time to renew his lease the landlord refused, saying that he wanted the store for one of his sons. Sam was forced to sell the store to the landlord. Undaunted, Sam moved to the small town of Bentonville, Arkansas. Based on the knowledge he obtained managing the Ben Franklin store, he started his own store.

Sam believed in constant improvement. Even though he had five stores in tiny towns with total revenues of over ten million dollars per year, which was incredible for the time period, he looked to IBM to incorporate relatively new computer technologies to better manage his stores.

He also believed that happy employees translated into

happy customers. Although he paid less wages than the industry average, he offered employees the ability to share in the company's success by offering a profit sharing program, where employees could buy stock in the company at a discount.

He also shared detailed performance information with employees, and entrusted employees, even clerks, with more responsibility than other retailers. All his employees were knowledgeable about the company's purchases, profits from sales, and were allowed to markdown prices to meet sale prices.

Sam also believed you had to learn from your competitors. He would not focus on what they doing wrong as most people do, but would focus on what they were doing right so he could incorporate those lessons into his own business and economic models.

Mr. Walton also was a contrarian. He would say that "If everyone is going one way there is a good chance you can find your niche by going in the opposite direction." Conventional wisdom says that opening a discount retail location requires a town with a population greater then 50 thousand. Target and Kmart ignored small towns, allowing Walmart to grow without competition for years.

Finally, Sam Walton said that to be successful you have to do what you love. He loved retail. For most people it is hard to get excited about the purchase of mundane items.

However, Sam loved the idea of taking an ordinary item, purchasing huge quantities of it, and then calling attention to it in his stores to make sales. To him it was a game he loved to play day in and day out. If you love what you do, working long hours is not a problem.

What takeaway lessons from Sam Walton's story resonate in your business?

Overcoming Your Fears
Dale Carnegie - Author

Dale Carnegie pretty much had a history of failing at every profession he tried. He tried farming, teaching, sales, acting, journalism, and even writing novels. Even his first marriage failed, and he never finished college. His long history of personal failures left him fascinated with the question of why some people were seemingly always successful. After some research he concluded that the key ingredient to success was self-confidence.

He learned that the only way to become self confident was to overcome your fears by confronting them head on. Being a very shy person, he decided to face his greatest fear and take on the subject of public speaking. He began lecturing his father's livestock. As he built some confidence he entered several debating contests. He lost. He kept at it anyway and soon got pretty good at debating and speaking in public.

He persuaded a local YMCA to allow him teach a course on public speaking. He wanted to earn $2.00 per night but the YMCA's management was hesitant, saying that they didn't feel his work was worth $2.00 per night, so he agreed on a straight commission. Soon he was earning $30.00 a night. He got his students to confront their fears and speak night after night. He wrote about what he learned from the experience in his first book, called The Art of Public Speaking, and started what we now call the self-help movement.

He postulated that healthy people don't write books about health; sick people who become interested in health write them. To him it made sense that people with the gift of dealing well with other people would not write How to Win Friends and Influence People. However, with his initial lack of experience in this area and his interest in learning more about subject, he could. The book went on to become a best seller.

Dale Carnegie also worried about everything and suffered from bouts of depression, so he researched the subject of worry and wrote another best seller called How to Stop Worrying and Start Living.

He understood that successful people identify their personal shortcomings and acquire the knowledge and skills needed to overcome them. It is personal improvement that makes you successful. Often we limit all that we can be based on our fears and lack of self-confidence. By a process of identifying your fears and making deliberate efforts to attack them, little by little you can achieve success and overcome your fears.

What are your shortcomings and fears, and what are you doing to overcome them?

Just Do It

Bill Bowerman - Nike

Bill Bowerman was a very successful track and field coach at the University of Oregon. Runners at the University often suffered from shinsplints, leg cramps, knee, and back issues as they trained. Bill was obsessed with designing solutions to solve these problems.

One morning he was in his kitchen watching his wife Barbara make waffles. As she removed a waffle from the waffle iron Bill took notice of the waffle's honey comb pattern, and was hit with an idea to produce a lightweight shock-absorbing shoe heel.

After breakfast he took her waffle iron to the garage, poured in some synthetic rubber, allowed it to cool, and cut out lightweight heel wedges that could be inserted into a running shoe. He then took them to the University and tested them out on his students.

Bill knew that shaving just one ounce of weight from a shoe translated into over 200 pounds less lifting force needed to run a single mile. Convinced there were huge applications for a shoe that incorporated a lightweight honeycomb shock-absorbing heel, he contacted several shoe manufacturers. None of the companies he contacted would agree to manufacture it.

As a coach Bill often told his students after they lost an event that "Losing can be a real beginning". He decided it was time to take his own advice and "Just do it", so he started his own shoe company. That company was Nike.

In addition to having the courage to follow his convictions and create a new category of footwear, the running shoe, to help draw attention to his new lightweight running shoe Bill wrote a book called Jogging. This introduced the public to the benefits of running, thereby creating a new industry.

Sometimes inspiration can come from the most unusual sources. When others can't see what it is that you see, maybe it is time to just do it. And finally, sometimes you have to write a book and show the world you're the expert to ignite a new industry.

Where do you find your inspiration?

Do you see solutions that others can't?

What are your plans to ignite a new industry around your idea?

The Golden Arches of Wisdom

Ray Kroc – McDonalds

Ray Kroc bought the rights to a small hamburger joint run by Dick and Mac McDonald. He was 52 years old at the time and selling milkshake machines. Ray always believed in the power of a positive attitude in sales. He said,

> *"With a smile and enthusiasm I can influence someone to buy a sundae when they came in for coffee."*

Ray also believed that as a salesperson you have to tailor your pitch or message to the needs of the customer. He said,

> *"Find out their taste and sell to it."*

In baseball, no pitcher throws the same pitch to every batter. Each batter prefers balls thrown to a particular part of the batting box and hits some types of pitches better than others. The same is true with each customer.

Most business start-ups need skills from more than their founder and take on partners. Sometimes these partners are less than the most desirable partners you might choose. This was no different for McDonalds. Ray had to take on an unwanted partner in the early stages of the business to get things moving in the right direction. Later in their history, Ray was in a position to buy out his unwanted partner.

Even though the unwanted partner and Ray often disagreed, he learned that to achieve success you don't want yes men surrounding you, but people willing to disagree with your position. In fact, Ray's initial franchise model was challenged by his executives. The resulting challenge allowed Ray to rethink his position and come up with the successful 'lease to own a store' franchise model.

Finally, Mr. Kroc knew that when it comes to expansion, it is best undertaken when times are bad so you can secure the best deals.

Ray Kroc was a man of modest upbringing and never even finished high school. He sold paper cups and milkshake machines and didn't even open his first McDonalds until he was in his 50s, yet he grew his net worth to over $500 million in less then 30 years, proving it is never too late to follow your entrepreneurial dreams.

Many lessons can be gleaned from Ray Kroc's story. What takeaway can you apply to your situation or business?

Bonus trivia: Ray Kroc was friends with Walt Disney when they served in the ambulance corp in World War I.

Challenge Conventional Wisdom

Walt Disney – The Walt Disney Company

Walt Disney took every challenge to his ideas as an opportunity to prove he was right.

Before Disney, cartoons were short animation films between 5-10 minutes in length that were shown before feature films. Walt Disney wanted to produce a full-length cartoon but everyone told him that no one would sit through a full-length cartoon. Taking up the challenge, he acted out the entire Snow White story winning over the skeptics in the audience. In 1937 Snow White and the Seven Dwarfs was released and became the first full length cartoon.

Walt Disney thought like an entrepreneur and understood that money was a tool. He had a grand vision to create a theme park called Disneyland that would feature all his charters. To fund his grand vision of creating Disneyland he created the TV program, The Wonderful World of Disney.

Disney invested heavily in himself. He was intellectually curious and was very much interested in acquiring knowledge for his own self improvement. He knew everyone has a story and sought out people from scientists to street sweepers, and asked them probing questions to learn about their jobs.

Walt Disney was dyslexic and his spelling and grammar were poor. However, most people who knew Walt Disney considered him the most educated man they knew.

Perseverance and courtesy lead us down new paths. Do you share some of the attributes of Walt Disney?

The Power of a Persons Name and Focus

Andrew Carnegie – Carnegie Steel

Andrew Carnegie was an industrialist who led the enormous expansion of the American steel industry. He knew that wealth came from creative thinking and not from hard work. Andrew spent six month a year traveling throughout Europe to have time to learn and reflect.

Andrew worked for the Pennsylvania Railroad as a telegraph operator. He rose rapidly in the company and learned about management and cost controls.

The railroad industry was a pretty corrupt industry, with lots of insider trading and payoff from contracts, and Andrew slowly accumulated some capital based on his investments. He invested $40k in a property in northwestern Pennsylvania that yielded over a $1m in cash dividends from oil.

On a trip to Europe he saw how blast furnace technology could be used in the making of steel. He knew that steel would replace wood as a structural component in construction, so he built a new plant in the US. However, he also knew that he needed to bring attention to his new steel plant.

Knowing the value a person places on their own name, he employed a rather ingenuous marketing technique. He named his new plant the Edger Thompson Works after the president of his former company, the Pennsylvania Railroad. Guess what: the trick resulted in him receiving his first order for 2000 rails.

Andrew Carnegie knew the value of leverage and knew he was not an expert, so he hired experts. He hired the top scientists and top accountants to make his business the best. As a result of his leveraging their expertise, the cost of rail was reduced from $160 per ton to just $17 per ton in less then 5 years, allowing him to realize huge profits.

He believed in being an inch wide and an mile deep and kept his focus on steel, never expanding into other areas.

The company always expanded in down markets, when labor and materials were cheapest. He coined the phrase,

> *"Keep your eggs in one basket and watch the basket"*.

Andrew Carnegie knew how to make money and became one of the greatest philanthropist of all time. Andrew Carnegie understood the power of a persons name and that focus is the key to success.

What can you learn from Andrew Carnegie's example?

Recognition on Steroids

Many Kay Ash – Mary Kay Cosmetics

We all know that negative effects can result from not appreciating your employees, as was the case with Benedict Arnold during the revolutionary war. On the opposite side of that same coin I would place Mary Kay Ash of Mary Kay Cosmetics. \

At the core of her business model was employee appreciation. She believed that it was vital to any business that supervisors go out of their way to recognize their workers. Even with over 850,000 employees, Ms. Ash sent each of her workers a PERSONAL birthday card. She believed for any recognition program to work you have to make it personal.

Mary Kay also believed that incentive programs needed to stand out and be first class because these programs tell people how important they are. To that end, she set up a very elaborate and generous "Thank You" system. Recognition ranged from a simple "Thank you for showing up early" to the iconic Pink Cadillac. Let's face it; Mary Kay's generous recognition program made huge network deposits on the employee side of the ledger. Employees were very eager to get back in balance by performing Herculean acts.

Moreover, Mary Kay Ash knew that people support efforts they help to create, so she frequently made it a habit to solicit input from her employees. Mary Kay Ash started her cosmetic empire with just $5,000 and an idea about how to keep people motivated, and turned it into an empire with over a billion dollars in sales.

Do you have a first class recognition program for your employees?

Constant Innovation

Charles Walgreen – Walgreens

What if you could give your customer his order before he was done giving it to you? Well, that idea is what built the drug store Walgreens.

When a nearby customer would call in a non-prescription order using the newly developed telephone, Charles Walgreen would repeat the caller's name, address and order so his assistant could hear it, and write down the address and the order. Then Charles would engage the customer in idle chit-chat while the assistant would grab the order off the shelf and race to the customer's home. While Charles was still on the phone his assistant would deliver the order, often before the customer was even off the phone with Charles.

Word soon spread about the exceptionally fast service Walgreen's pharmacy delivered. These stunts and other innovations propelled Walgreens from a small Chicago pharmacy into a $24.6 billion dollar, 3,520 store business.

Carbonated water was used in the pharmacy business in the early 1900s. Many pharmacies bottled the soda water with added flavoring as a health aid. Charles saw another opportunity. Why not add a soda fountain and a bar and tables where people could sit? It was a hit. So he then added ice cream and sundaes to his offerings, which also turned out to be a hit.

But serving ice cream was not enough. It didn't create enough differentiation from other pharmacies, so Charles developed a private label premium ice cream that contained more butterfat, creating a higher quality product offering.

While sales soared in the summer, as fall turned into winter the demand for ice cream began to wain. Charles, the consummate tinkerer, examined the situation and added hot soup, sandwiches, and desserts, and sales rose again.

When summer returned he again examined the situation. With the help of his fountain manger he developed the milkshake, which turned into yet another hit.

In the following years he added a perfume bar so women could sample perfumes before they bought them. This was another first which turned out to be successful. Then he added a cigar and pipe tobacco bar for men.

Knowing that customers wanted to save money, but also knowing that running too many sales made you look cheap, he reached out to other local pharmacies and created the Valet Club. Through the Valet Club the pharmacies could collectively negotiate lower prices from suppliers. For example, a Gillette razor that usually sold for $1.00 sold at Walgreens for only $.69 because of the volume purchasing power of the Valet Club members.

Charles Walgreen was a constant innovator who was never happy with the status quo. He kept his mind open so he could spot new ideas.

How can you think more like Charles Walgreen and expand your product or service offerings to stay ahead of the competition?

A Lesson in Perseverance

John Johnson – Ebony Magazine

John Johnson grew up in a small shack with a tin roof in rural Arkansas. In an effort to give John more opportunities, his family moved to Chicago when he was 15 years old. However, coming from a poor area in Arkansas, his new classmates made fun of his accent and handmade clothes.

To deal with his unpleasant school situation John turned to self-help books. He was inspired by the lessons from Dale Carnegie in dealing with adversity and unpleasant things. Drawing on his experience of growing up black in the 1930s and 40s, and the lessons learned from Carnegie and other self-help writers, John decided that he wanted to start a magazine called Ebony to highlight successes in the black community.

John figured he would need about $500 to fund the creation of Ebony magazine. When he went to his local bank he was told they could not give him a loan because he was black. Undaunted, he asked the loan officer where he might get the funding he needed. However, rather then just come out and ask the loan office who else he could call on, he used the self-help lessons he had learned and framed the question in such a way that it was in the interest of the loan officer to provide a qualified lead. His strategy worked; the loan officer even agreed to provide John with an introduction, and he finally secured his start up funds. A little while later when he wanted an interview with the first lady, Eleanor Roosevelt, he was denied based upon her time constraints. Rather then move on, he persevered and continued his correspondence with Eleanor's office. When he learned she was passing through Chicago he asked if she had the time to simply dictate a column for his magazine. It worked, she agreed, and with the article his circulation doubled.

Later when John wanted an interview with Eugene McDonald, the CEO of Zenith Radio, he did some research on McDonald and learned he was an arctic explorer. John secured a copy of the book *"A Negro Explorer at the North Pole"* signed by Matthew Henson, Admiral Robert Peary's black assistant. While McDonald initially consented to the interview, he said there was no way he would advertise in Johnson's magazine. During the interview Johnson presented Eugene with the autographed copy of the book and said his goal with the Ebony magazine was to highlight black success. Mr. McDonald was so touched by the gesture of the book he said "You know, I don't see any reason why we shouldn't advertise in this magazine" without ever even being asked.

John Johnson knew that you had to tell people what was in it for them and they would happily help you achieve your objectives.

Page 25

Do you know a person's interest and sell your solutions to it?

Do you take no for an answer, or do you keep looking for ways to accomplish your objectives?

Build an Empire, Bowl by Bowl

Brownie Wise - Tupperware

Earl Tupper invented Tupperware but he had a hard time selling it. People didn't trust plastic, and they didn't know how to use the product he developed to store items in air-tight containers.

His sales for his first six years was essentially flat. Moreover, he was an introvert and could not manage a sales force like many other inventors. Enter Miss Brownie Wise. She said that the only way to sell a product like Tupperware was through demonstrations, and the Tupperware party was born.

Brownie was a struggling divorcee raising a sick child as a single mom. Her first attempt to sell Tupperware at a party was an utter disaster. She was so nervous she became physically nauseated during the presentation and tripped over her own display, hitting her face on the floor. She was forced to leave the house with a bloody nose; absolutely the worst nightmare you could imagine. Her next few parties were not much better. However, even though her son was in the hospital she persevered and continued to give Tupperware parties.

Earlier Brownie had taken a Dale Carnegie course. She

knew that she just had to keep at it and just like Dale's experience told her, it would one day lead to success. Eventually she got better and was soon selling two truckloads of product a week as an independent dealer.

Earl Tupper was so impressed with her success that he knew he had to hire her to build his sales force. Brownie remembered her rocky start and never judged a book by its cover. She gave everyone a chance to be a Tupperware salesperson and ruled no one out. She knew that if you build people up they will help you build your business.

Everyone was a customer to Brownie. Once a gas station attendant saw her product in the back of her car. Before she left the filling station she had arranged to have his wife host a Tupperware party.

Wise knew that to be successful you also had to be goal oriented. Her first goal was to buy a house. To reinforce this goal she cut out a picture of a house like the one she coveted and hung it on the wall where she could see it every day.

She believed you have to plan for small victories every day and monitor your progress toward your goal. If you can't see your progress, many people become impatient. They simply abandon their goals. You have to create a chart and plot your progress so you can keep focused on your goal. In 1951 there were 200 Tupperware dealers. By 1954, a mere three years later, there were 9,000 dealers.

The deck was stacked against Brownie from the start but she persevered and became a huge success.

How can you internalize the lessons from Brownie Wise and implement them in your business?

Welfare to Entrepreneur

Daisy Braxton - Superior Janitorial Services

Daisy Braxton was a single mom with five children when she lost her job. To make ends meet she worked several minimum wage jobs that didn't offer healthcare. Soon, medical bills for her kids overwhelmed her, and she was forced to apply for welfare.

Rather than begin a lifelong dependency on the government, she took a course on janitorial work the welfare center offered. After working for a janitorial contracting company for about two years to learn about the business, she decided to started her own cleaning company.

The first year was rough and she made only $45k. However, each year was better than the previous one. She knew that quality sold, so she provided detailed procedures to each of her employees that they were required to follow to the letter. Before the job was done a supervisor had to check every detail. Soon the word began to spread about her company's quality work and the company that was hired by the welfare center to train her in janitorial work asked her to teach others.

While training others she kept her eyes and ears open and learned about new contract opportunities for her company.

Being a trainer, she also had access to a steady workforce of new workers from her class and the welfare rolls.

New workers were first assigned to clean empty buildings where they could not damage the brand if they didn't work out before moving up to clean private homes.

With a scalable business and economic model, Daisy could focus on making new sales. Daisy took advantage of a training opportunity while on welfare and parlayed it into a very successful business by persevering and keeping her eyes open to new opportunities. She learned about the industry by working as an employee before taking the leap. Daisy's story is not that unique.

Are you able to spot opportunities when they are presented to you?

Are you willing to take the appropriate actions to make them a reality?

Have a Coke and a Smile

Robert Woodruff - Coke-Cola

Robert Woodruff was a truck salesman who got poor grades in school, but by 34 he became the CEO of Coca Cola and turned a pharmacy elixir into one of America's best known consumer brands. How did he do it? By focusing on keeping customers happy and making the drink the best it could be through consistency.

One day as a new CEO he called all his salespeople together and told them they were all fired. He went on to say that the company had created some new positions and anyone interested could attend a meeting the following day and apply for some of the new jobs.

You can imagine the conversations that went on that night. The next day Robert said the new role was that of "serviceman", stressing that service to customers was now job number one. The drama of the firing and a night to think about it made the message stick.

Next he took a tour of the bottling plant. He noticed broken glass behind machines and dust and sticky syrup just about everywhere. He instructed the plant manager to have the entire plant cleaned top to bottom by morning or find another job. The plant manager protested, saying it would not do any good to clean everything because the bottling process was messy, and the plant would look the same by the end of the day tomorrow. Undaunted, Mr. Woodruff told him "You wipe you ass don't you," and walked out.

To improve the consistency to the consumer he then set up a fountain drink training school. The program stressed that the product had to be served at exactly 34 degrees, had to be served with crushed ice, and had to be served in a specially designed bell-shaped glass for optimum flavor.

Robert Woodruff knew that he had a good product, but to grow as a business Coca Cola had to make sure both that the product quality was first rate and that the customer experience was consistent.

Next, he made sure all trucks were the same red color and even standardized the drivers' uniforms. He made sure advertising was consistent.

Robert Woodruff understood the power of a dramatic effect to make a message stick. He knew that success lay in customer perception, and that customer perception would ultimately drive customer demand.

Do you use dramatic effect to make people remember?

How focused is your business on the customer experience?

Who Will Destroy Me Today?

Arthur Blank – The Home Depot

Arthur Blank, one of the founders of Home Depot, wakes up every morning saying

> *"Who will destroy me today if I don't keep my eyes open."*

Knowing that retailers can't sit still or they'll be eclipse by the competition, Arthur Blank and Bernie Marcus started Home Depot after being laid off unexpectedly from Handy Dan Home Improvement.

Rather than follow the standard hardware store model, they looked outside the box and envisioned a huge warehouse store for the Do-It-Yourself person. They figured that rather than make separate trips to plumbing suppliers, electric suppliers, lumber yards, and so on to complete a home remodeling job, customers would prefer a one stop warehouse with many departments.

Moreover, rather than hiring salespeople, they visualized hiring tradespeople with real life experience to man the different departments. And not only would these workers be paid in salary; they also would receive stock options so they would have a vested interest in the company's success.

The plan worked. At Home Depot payroll is not considered an expense but an investment. The strategy payed off so well that management had to develop policies to limit managers from working more then 55 hours per week because they became so dedicated to their stores' success.

Also no one, not even executives working for headquarters, can work without first working in a store. This keeps the focus on the store and not on headquarters. Even vendors at Home Depot are encouraged to strap on the orange and work the floor to better understand the customers.

Successful entrepreneurs know that you always have to keep you eyes open and constantly need to look at new ideas to separate you from the competition.

What are you doing to keep one step ahead of your competition?

Not Enough White, Too Much Purple

Charles Tandy – RadioShack

Tandy Leather was a family owned business located in Texas. Dave Tandy was a partner in a leather heel and shoe repair business which was founded in 1919. Charles Tandy, the son of Dave, took over the business after World War II and changed the business's focus to leather craft after seeing how leather crafts were being used as therapy for injured solders.

Charles learned many valuable lessons during these early years. When a leather dye company offered to sell him 10 different dye colors, Charles bought an inventory of all 10 colors. Soon all of the white dye was sold, but he had nearly all his purple inventory left. The first lesson he learned was to think about your inventory and track your sales. Do you have not enough white and too much purple?

Next, Charles saw how his dad and his partner worked tirelessly on the business. Lesson number two was ownership means the owners will work extra hours– not for you or the company, but for themselves because their money is at risk.

Tandy Leather was acquired in 1956 by General American Industries (GAI), but GAI lacked a cohesive direction which soon began a power struggle. Leveraging his resources, Charles raised additional money and exercised his stock options to successfully take control of GAI. The name of the company was changed to the Tandy Corporation and the company continued to sell craft supplies under Charles's leadership.

By 1961, the Tandy Corporation operated 125 stores and had a thriving mail order business. Lesson number three was to track your mail order sales to discover where your customers live. After discovering where your customers live, go to that city and find an intersection that everyone in town knows. Keep walking around in ever increasing circles until you can afford the rent to open up a new store.

However, in spite of operating 125 stores, Charles was looking for a new edge and began looking at the electronic craft industry. Charles became convinced that the do-it-yourself movement was gaining momentum and spotted an opportunity.

The year was 1963. Radio Shack operated 9 stores, but was on the verge of bankruptcy. Charles Tandy studied Radio Shack for over 6 months and figured that their issues were all related to poor management. Tandy spoke to his board of directors, saying he wanted to buy Radio Shack. The board was not convinced.

Charles was so sure the electronic hobby space was the next frontier that he decided the only course of action was to play hardball. He said he would sell all his Tandy stock and do it alone if the board didn't agree. The board knew if Charles sold all his stock, it would cripple the Tandy corporation so they reluctantly agreed to buy Radio Shack. Lesson number four was sometimes people don't share your vision and you have to be willing to go it alone if need be.

Although Charles knew nothing about electronics when he acquired Radio Shack, he grew the business to its height in the year 2000 to over 7,100 stores and over 4.8 billion dollars in sales. Lesson number five was vendors who are not getting your business are much more anxious and motivated to give you their best price.

Business owners can learn a lot from Charles Tandy's experience.

Do you track your sales to see what is hot and what is not?

Do you enjoy the tireless effort from multiple equity partners?

How will you locate your next new store?

How far are you willing to go to convince others you are right?

Are you aware of the vendors that would desperately love to be your supplier?

Facts and Science Rule

William Boeing - Boeing

Basing business decisions on science and facts should be paramount to any entrepreneur. No one epitomizes this philosophy more the William Boeing.

William Boeing was born into a family owned lumber business. However, he attended an air show in 1910 and he knew aviation would bring a sea-change to the transportation industry.

As an engineer, he believed that engineering as a science should be at the core of a company's success. Since early airplanes used wood framing and fabric for their skins, his lumber business was in a good position to build planes.

After seeing one of the first boxy hydroplanes, he knew he could design a much better plane. Needing a place to test his designs, he paid for the construction of a newly invented wind tunnel at the University of Washington's campus. In exchange for the new wind tunnel, Boeing requested that the university develop a curriculum in the new field of aeronautics so they would turn out engineers for his business.

William believed that decisions should be based strictly on

fact and not opinions. In fact, a placard on the wall of his outer office read:

1. There is no authority except facts.
2. Facts are obtained by accurate observation.
3. Deductions are to be made only from facts.
4. Experience has proved the truth of these rules.

If the facts said something could be done, then he refused to listen to so-called experts that said otherwise. For example, Boeing went on to build sea planes for the Navy during WWI. However, once WWI ended, the market for planes significantly decreased and many experts recommended that Boeing close his aviation business, saying that aviation would be nothing more than an expensive joyride.

Boeing did not take these experts advice since his data proved otherwise. He even used his own personal wealth to keep engineering new planes even when there were few orders. To keep the company afloat during this tenuous time after WWI, he used the lumber he might have used to build airplanes to instead build furniture.

Nine years after WWI ended, the United States Postal Service (USPS) was looking for bids to carry mail by air. Boeing examined ways to profitably carry mail for the USPS. His data showed he could make a profit on the Chicago to San Francisco route. Boeing's bid was two thirds the rate of the other bids. Experts said air mail was just too costly to be profitable. Even the USPS doubted his bid and required Boeing to post a bond to get the contract.

What the competitors didn't account for was the weight of the plane itself. Boeing knew he could build a lighter airplane by using an air cooled engine rather than the traditional water cooled engine. The decision proved to be very successful and profitable for Boeing.

William Boeing never accepted "it can't be done" and instead said "keep researching and experimenting to lick what appear to be insurmountable difficulties."

Do you take no for an answer or do continue to conduct research to gather the facts to find a solution that so-called experts say can't be done?

Never Get Too Comfortable

Jorma Ollila - Nokia

Sometimes managers get too comfortable with their jobs and build internal walls to control knowledge in the hopes of making them indispensable to the company. The result is the company begins to stagnate.

To combat this thinking and spur innovation, Jorma Ollila, CEO of Nokia, implemented a job swap program. Nokia adopted an everyone-out-of-your-comfort-zone management style and regularly practiced managerial musical chairs to keep the company fresh and breaking down silos.

This practice created a certain amount of chaos and a sense of urgency, forcing managers to learn from each other as they learned how the other half worked. This practice, although a risky gamble, payed off for Nokia as it went from ten billion in revenue in 1997 to over twenty billion in just 2 years and assuming the #1 spot in the wireless phone industry by 1999.

In another move to unlock the company's potential, Nokia encouraged its workers to meet in unusual places to spur creativity. My company did the documentation for Nokia during this time frame and during a meeting with several executives in Finland, our team was loaded onto a few dogsleds and whisked off to a remote cabin for a meeting. While I personally did not make this trip, I remember their stories and learned that sled dogs pooped and peed while running, creating a rather memorable ride for them.

Sometimes you have to take deliberate actions, perhaps unpopular ones, to get the best from employees and managers.

What can you do to shake things up in your business?

Size Up a Business in Less than 5 Minutes
John Chambers – Cisco Systems

John Chambers, former CEO of Cisco Systems, says he can size up a business, determine their culture, and determine whether or not they are customer focused in less than 5 minutes. Chambers should know because he acquired scores of companies to grow Cisco systems into one of the top computer networking players.

First, he looks at the location of the offices. He looks to see if the employees are out where the natural light is and if the offices of the managers are located toward the middle. Office size and location shows if a company's commitment is more to enrich managers or support employees where the real work gets done.

Next, he looks at the type of furniture that is in the office. High end offices with rich mahogany furniture says that the business is too internally focused. Chambers likes to see plain furniture, which shows that the business is more frugal.

He then looks to see if employees are tied to the success of the business in some way such as having stock options. If there are stock options, he also looks to see how they are distributed between employees and managers to determine the culture.

Finally, John Chambers says you can learn a lot about a company by what it places on the walls. He looks to see what is important to them. For instance, are there pictures of family, sporting events, and other outings or is there just some store bought art with little meaning? Sizing up a business, whether as a potential vendor or acquisition target, can tell you a lot about their customer focus and culture.

What does your office say about you?

Pivot, Pivot, Pivot

Pierre Omidyar - eBay

The year was 1995 and Pierre Omidyar wanted to help his girlfriend trade Pez candy dispensers. He was working as an engineer for General Magic Inc. in the San Francisco Bay Area. In his personal time, he created "Auction Web," a site that served as a neighborhood community for sellers and buyers to meet. At first, he charged users a small fee to post their goods on the site. It didn't take long for buyer and sellers to discover the site. Within a few months, the traffic got the attention of his ISP, which demanded he upgrade his service.

Astonished by its success, Omidyar wrote some code and set up a new site devoted to auctions. Still believing it was just a local community-based trading platform for the San Francisco bay area, he named it eBay. He charged sellers anywhere from $.25 to $2.00 to post an item for sale and collected a commission of 1.25% to 5% on successful sales. Less than 9 months in, Pierre Omidyar quit his day job to focus on eBay full time.

His little community-based trading platform started to encompass sellers and buyers from all over the world. By 1997, the sales growth was astonishing and exceeded 1,400%. Benchmark Capital valued the company at $100 million and invested $22 million for a 22% stake in the business to take the company public in 1998.

As the appointed Chairman, Pierre turned over the day to day business operations to Med Whitman, who set up the "eBay Cafe" and "Feedback Forum" to solicit feedback from customers.

Omidyar soon acquired Half.com so it could offer set-price trading and made customer service available 24/7.

Small business owners can learn a lot from Pierre Omidyar and the birth of eBay. Big businesses can start from humble beginnings. Omidyar started the business based on a perceived problem, the lack of a platform to trade Pez dispensers. He kept his day job while he experimented to find the right value proposition, revenue strategy, posting charges, and back-end commissions on sales. Sometimes a solution that works for a small niche, the Bay Area, has much larger applications. Soliciting feedback from users allowed him to continue to meet and exceed the expectations of his users.

How can you use the lessons learned from Pierre Omidyar in your business?

Ask Your Customer What They Think

Meg Whitman - eBay

"The year was 1998 and eBay was little more than a glorified flea market with 6 million in sales", recalls Meg Whitman when she became eBay's CEO. Three years later eBay had $748 million in sales and 62 million registered users, becoming the envy of the dot-com world.

Whitman attributes this growth to persistence and vision, but her real success is based on quickly spotting trends and listening to customers.

When a new product category sprouted legs, she played it up to ensure maximum buzz on user bulletin boards. She also made it a rule to constantly work user inputs into daily operations.

Several times a year she would fly customers to eBay headquarters to get their take on ideas. A few weeks later she would follow up with conference calls to fine tune the ideas before they were implemented.

Whitman explains,

"The users are our company since they are the ones who bring the product and merchandise it."

She knew that the more options users have, the more often they return.

In 2002, one of these ideas led to the expansion of fixed prices, providing an alternative to those who would rather buy without bidding.

As the CEO, she set big goals and developed strategies to get there. It was this thinking that led to eBay buying out Pay-Pal to reduce their processing costs.

What lessons from Meg Whitman and eBay can you apply to your business?

A Better Path to the Customer

Steve Case – AOL

The year was 1990. Microsoft just released it's first successful version of the Windows Operating System. The TCP/IP protocol went global and the internet was now within reach of users with a personal computer in their home.

Prodigy just went public and launched a marketing campaign with a war-chest worth nearly a billion dollars and were backed by IBM and Sears. By contrast, Steve Case of America OnLine (AOL) had 1 million in venture capital and knew he could not compete directly with Prodigy or CompuServe, the current leaders in the the industry, so he looked for a better strategy.

Most internet users during this time were tech savvy early adopters. Rather than try and compete in that market, Steve made the decision to focus on people unfamiliar with computers. AOL instead chose to spend its venture money to mail their AOL internet start up disks directly to people's homes. Additionally, AOL struck deals with major airlines to distribute their AOL disks to passengers.

This tactic worked and by the mid-1990's, AOL surpassed Prodigy and CompuServe, becoming the leading internet service provider.

The lesson for the entrepreneur is that you don't have to be the first mover nor have a huge marketing budget to become the preeminent leader in your industry. All it takes is for you to look for a better path to the customer.

Are you stuck trading blows with your competitors or are you looking for a better path to your customer?

Customer Service Is More than a Slogan

Mickey Drexler - The Gap Inc.

Mickey Drexler hates emails and memos, but loves to communicate face to face or over the phone. He prefers personal interactions so he can be sure that others are listening to him.

When Drexler was hired as the new president of Gap Inc's Stores Division in 1983, his first order of business was to fire everyone in the complaint division because they took six weeks to respond to complaints. He states that every person in the company was now the complaint department.

When Drexler joined Gap Inc, its three stores brands (The Gap, Banana Republic, and Old Navy) had only 550 stores and was in deep trouble. By the mid 2000's, they had 4,250 stores and Drexler had built the clothing retailer into a nine billion dollar a year business by simply making customer service more than a slogan. "Think and act like the customer" is Gap Inc's operating motto.

The company uses two-way communication between customers and staff as well as between employees and management. Drexler is always open to speaking to customers in stores, in elevators, or wherever. He has even been known to stop and ask 12 year old kids on the street about his product line.

The result of all this communication helped Gap Inc. changed their clothing lines from upscale clothes that were not selling well to simple, more casual clothes. Drexler likes to say that he invented "Casual Friday".

He knows that a customer's first exposure to the chains clothing is with the window display so he paid particular attention to them. Thinking like the customer, he made sure signs were readable and instructed his employees to made sure that they would greet a customer within 30 seconds of entering the department.

To keep up with employees, Drexler would start calling them as early as 6:30 while he was working out on his treadmill. If they were not there, he would leave them a lengthy voice mail message they could not ignore. Instead of meeting behind closed doors, he preferred to meet in the hallway so he could respond quickly and foster an atmosphere of openness.

Mickey Drexler was focused on thinking like the customer and that communications needed to be person to person in real time.

What can you learn from Mickey Drexler that you can apply to your business?

Starbuck's Secret Sauce

Howard Schultz – Starbucks

When Howard Schultz of Starbucks is having a bad day, he digs his hands into a barrel of coffee and breaths in deeply. He is then reminded of why he got into the business in the first place – For the love of coffee.

Schultz has learned that you need a trick to get your passion back when you are having a rough time. Schultz learned this lesson when he was growing up and watching the Beatles. As they became more and more popular, "they could no longer hear their own music. He would say, "They forgot what they stood for."

In 1987, Howard and a few investors purchased a Seattle coffee house and built it into the market leader it is today by introducing Americans to Europe's romance with gourmet coffee. By 2002, Starbucks had grown from one store to 5,689 stores, operated in 28 countries, and experienced the highest annual growth rate of any retailer.

Yet, sniffing coffee is not Schultz's only secret to building a great company. Here are 6 others:

1. Arrive one hour early to critical meetings and walk around the block to calm yourself down and

practice your presentation.

2. Speak, do not read in public. Even if you are a skilled orator you will sound canned and passionless if you read your presentation. If you are afraid you'll forget what to say, write 3 or 4 words on 3x5 index cards before the presentation to stay on point. Finally, tell lots of stories; people are hungry for human contact and are attracted to something they can relate to.

3. Remember that when you hire someone, you are hiring more than their labor. You are also hiring the baggage they bring with them.

4. Be vulnerable. Schultz has cried in front of employees and has opened up about his fears. He says there is no better way to show honesty than by exposing your fears. He says honesty is the top ingredient of success.

5. Be upbeat. Don't candy coat bad news, but leaders must be optimistic. Business leaders have the intuitive sense that things will work out for the best and do not see the dark side. Go into every situation assuming that you will win and it will give you the courage to take chances.

6. Build a memorable experience by reading and giving into your curiosity. If you attend a seminar, read a book or two on the topic to solidify the knowledge. When Schultz visited the FDR memorial in Washington, he read several books on the Great Depression to feed his curiosity and make the experience more memorable.

There are many lesson business owners can learn from Howard Schultz. Which lesson from Howard Schultz can you apply today?

Timing Is Everything

Samuel Colt – Colt's Manufacturing Company

As a hunter and gun enthusiast, I admire the inventor of the revolver, Samuel Colt. Prior to the revolver, the American armed forces used the muzzle loader. While the muzzle loader was a powerful weapon that could extend the lethal range of a soldier, it was a single shot weapon and took time to reload. In the time it took to reload a muzzle loader, an Indian could fire many arrows, leaving the soldiers at a disadvantage after the first volley of shots were fired.

While a gun with at rotating cylinder had already been invented, the cylinder had to be rotated by hand. With the newly devised percussion cap, Sam Colt, who was an able bodied seaman at the time, whittled a prototype out of wood while out at sea. Sam's design allowed the act of pulling the hammer back not only to cock the gun, but also to rotate the cylinder and align the next bullet.

The timing of Colt's idea could not have come at a better time. As Sam was preparing to demonstrate his new weapon, the massacre at the Alamo took place and the military desperately wanted a repeating gun to tilt the war to their advantage. Sam used the opportunity and went to Washington DC to lobby for his invention. He talked to anyone that would listen and he would often talk and drink with influential figures into the wee hours of the morning.

Ultimately, his partners did not see the direct results in sales that they had hoped for. They felt Sam was hobnobbing and partying at their expense. As a result, the company partners decided to split up, leaving Colt without access to a production facility.

Always a man seeking self improvement, Sam befriended Sam Morse, the investor of the telegraph. Sam Morse convinced Colt that he needed to pay for good press to promote his invention. So Sam went to the Texas Rangers and got a testimonial from Sam Walker, the famous Texas Ranger. With Walker's help, Colt redesign his revolver and created the iconic "Walker 44," the largest and most powerful black powder repeating handgun ever made.

It was very well received, but as orders came in to put it into production, Sam didn't have a factory to produce them. Without a production facility, Sam contracted Eli Whitney, who invented the cotton gin, to build his revolver. With the success of the initial run he was able to attract new investors and eventually went on to build his own production facility.

He also continued to woo politicians and the media for the rest of his life as he focused on making the perfect gun.

Over time, production improvements at his plant lowered the cost of his guns, making them affordable for the average American. This improvement occurred just as the Great Westward Expansion was taking place after the Civil War.

Sam Colt was not only a great marketer; he was also a man who never gave up on his idea even in the face of adversity. He ultimately achieved great economies of scale when the market timing was right. Sometimes the market needs to come to you as was the case with Sam Colt's revolver changed the nature of war and tamed the Wild West.

What lessons from Sam Colt can you apply to your business?

Lessons from the First Black Woman Millionaire

C.J. Walker – Walker Manufacturing Company

As the Director of Entrepreneurship at a local community college, we offer a student success course base on the eight life lessons passed on to Clifton Taulbert from his uncle Cleve Morman from the book "Who Owns The Ice House, Eight Lesson from An Unlikely Entrepreneur."

An equally impressive story comes from Madame C.J. Walker (a.k.a. Sarah Breedlove), the first black woman millionaire.

She was born to slaves and worked the cotton fields in Louisiana. At age seven, she was orphaned and forced to move in with an older sister. At age fourteen, she married to escape the mistreatment from her sister's husband. At seventeen, she had a daughter. At age 20, her husband died, forcing her to move to St. Louis where her three brothers lived.

Her brothers were all barbers and she took a job as a washer woman where she earned about one dollar per day. As if things were not bad enough, she suffered from a common problem affecting black women of her day: hair loss. This hair loss was most likely a symptom of her poor diet and the harsh chemicals black women often used to their clear hair.

She learned about hair care from her brothers and became a commissioned sales agent for an African American hair care entrepreneur named Annie Malone.

While working for Annie, she added to her knowledge of hair care, but knew that Annie's product was not quite right. However, rather than reinvent the wheel, she added several vitamins and minerals known to promote healthy hair and created a new formula. By using the product herself, she saw her own hair return to its original thickness and knew her formula was more effective.

Even though she was a domestic servant in the early 1900's with little to no hope of advancement, she longed for a life of financial independence. She began to think what life would be like if she could sell her new hair care solution.

Although she was illiterate, she had a knack for marketing. She knew she wanted to sell the product to as many black woman as possible. Since most blacks like her could not read, advertising was out of the question. She also knew that few blacks would trust a white sales person so she decided to operate her business using only black women selling to other black women.

Marketing was a primitive science back then and sales calls primary involved the use of high-pressure tactics to sell a product to people who really did not need it. Instead, she tailored her product and distribution network to her customer's needs and believed in selling by example.

She had all her sales gals dress in black skirts and white shirts and emphasized "cleanliness and loveliness." Walking through a neighborhood, her "Walker Agents," as they we called, were recognizable in their uniforms and sparkling hygiene.

When most black women toiled in menial labor, Walker's Agents gave them a ray of hope. Walker realized that economic emancipation was a one way a black woman could break out of the cycle of discrimination and economic abuse so she compensated her agents very well.

Walker didn't let life dictate her future, she developed a goal, navigated the obstacles in her way, and never quit. Being illiterate did not stop her. Rather, it forced her to look at other solutions.

What lesson can you take away from Walker's story?

How can you use your situation to look at life in a way that may be foreign to others?

Keep Trying Until You Get It Right

Malcom McLean – Sea-Land Company

After graduating high school, Malcom McLean bought a used truck and started a small trucking company with his sister and brother. Two years later in 1937, Malcom found himself sitting in a long line of trucks on the Hoboken, NJ docks. He was awaiting his turn for the stevedores and longshoreman to unload his cargo of cotton and place the bails in cargo nets to manually load into the hold of each ship.

This century old process, known as break bulk shipments, involved manually loading and unloading cargo from manufacturer to truck, truck to ship, ship to truck, and finally, truck to destination. This process was a colossal waste of time and manpower.

As Malcom waited for his turn, he thought there must be a better way. It dawned on him that sorting and packaging goods into large containers for shipment would make the process faster, safer, and cheaper.

Years passed as he considered the idea further. By early 1950, he developed a plan to ship his entire loaded truck on a trailer ship., However, it proved impractical since the ship's hull is curved and box trucks are rectangular, leaving a large quantity of wasted cargo space between the truck's sides and the ship's curved bulkheads below decks. Moreover, the cab, engine, and wheels also contributed to more wasted space.

Finally in 1955, he revised his concept to loading just the container or box and not the truck's chassis. Since interstate commission regulations prevented a trucking company from also being a shipping company, Malcom decided to sell his share of McLean trucking and used the money to buy the Pan Atlantic Steamship Company for the operating rights to carry containers by ship.

He also bought the Gulf Florida Terminal Company, which he fitted with gantry cranes to load the containers on to ships. He then secured a loan to purchase two WWII tanker ships, which he extensively modified to carry containers both on and under the decks.

In 1956, the cost to load and unload cargo from ships employed thousands of stevedores and longshoremen, costing an average of $5.86 per ton. With McLean's new containerized shipment, it cost only 16 cents per ton or less than 1/36th the cost. Not only did it cost less to load and unload, it also took much less time. Since ships and trucks only make money when they were moving, trucking and shipping companies loved the idea and the Sea-Land Company was born.

McLean took almost 18 years to realize his idea. He

continued to use his trucking company to generate the profits he could later use to build the Sea-Land Company. The technology of containerized shipments displaced an entire industry of dock workers who were not happy.

How can you use the lessons from Malcom McLean and apply them to your ideas and business?

Barbie, Seeing Things Others Do Not

Elliot & Ruth Handler – Mattel

Izzy (later change to Elliot) and Ruth Handler were husband and wife that complemented each other's skills when it came to business. Elliot was the dreamer, who I have often refer to in business as the Oracle or someone who can see things that other can not. Ruth, by contrast, had a business mind and is what I like to call the General.

They had two kids named Barb and Ken. Together Elliot and Ruth started a toy company they called Mattel. Elliot's first product inspiration was that of a plastic ukulele, which was closely followed by a toy piano. Since they were short of capital, Ruth and Elliot would attend toy fairs where store buyers would go to sell their new toy ideas.

Even though they had successful products, the Handler's lost money since they were relatively inexperienced in manufacturing and distribution. They underestimated their costs, which significantly ate into their margins. Even though the musical toys sold over 20 million units, there was no margin that the company could use to grow. They figured they had to go big or go home. They figured that if you are going to drive off the cliff, it is better to leave no skid marks.

Up until that point in time, toys were not marketed to kids, but to parents. While this practice seems incredibly short sighted today, no one thought to market products to children at the time.

There was a new TV show ready to début. Mattel bet the farm and agreed to become a sponsor for the new show. The show was called "The Wonderful World of Disney" and proved to be a big hit, especially with kids.

The first product that Mattel was marketing on the TV show was a Burp Gun, a toy that made a burping sound instead of a bang when the child pulled the trigger. Since the audience of the show was kids, it was the first time marketers focused on selling directly to kids and not to their parents. Being a sponsor of "The Wonderful World of Disney" proved to be a brilliant move and the company's revenue grew three fold almost overnight.

Elliot and Ruth took at trip to Switzerland with their kids Barb and Ken. At one store, they saw an adult doll dressed in a work cloths. The doll was not a kid's toy, but was marketed to adults. Up to that time, all dolls marketed to young girls were babies so that the girl could pretend that she was the doll's mommy. As Barb handled the doll, the Handler's got an idea. More and more woman were entering the workforce so why not develop a doll where the child could pretend to be a career girl and an adult rather than just a mom. They tried to buy one doll and several outfits, but the store owner said there was only one outfit for each doll and the outfits were not interchangeable.

The Handler's asked themselves, "What if girls could buy one doll and many outfits to accessorize the doll to fit various scenarios?" The Barbie doll was born. With the launch of the Barbie doll, Mattel went on to be a major player in the toy market.

Statically, the average American girl growing up owned upwards of 10 Barbie dolls along with all the accessories that came with them.

Elliot and Ruth where a great pair; one was the Oracle, the other was the General. Their first products, while very successful, made them little money as they learned about margin the hard way. When they faced a cross road, they went all in and hit a home run by sponsoring a children's show. They were not afraid to go against the conventional wisdom of the day, which included marketing toys only to parents and making only baby dolls.

What lesson from Elliot and Ruth Handler can you use in your business?

Chapter 2: The Titans of Industry

The dawn of the 20th century saw incredible growth and prosperity in American industry. Four leaders emerged that grew their businesses from humble beginnings to become the dormant forces in their industries. These four icons have become know as the titan of industry and consist of:

- Cornelius Vanderbilt

- John D. Rockefeller

- Andrew Carnegie

- J. Pierpont Morgan

Some called them robber barons and other ruthless cutthroats, but for the entrepreneur each has valuable business lessons.

Lessons from the Shipping Tycoon Cornelius Vanderbilt

Cornelius Vanderbilt quit school at age 11 and began working on one of his father's ferries. By the time he was 16, he decided to start his own ferry business and bought a shallow draft two masted sailing ship to ferry freight and passengers between Manhattan Island and Staten Island, New York.

After saving his money, he bought his brother-in-law's schooner and added it to his fleet. His energy and entrepreneurial spirit at such a young age caught the attention of Thomas Gibbons, who owned a steamboat enterprise. His entrepreneurial spirit also earned young Vanderbilt the nickname of "Commodore."

Vanderbilt watched as Gibbons went all the way to the the Supreme Court to overturn the steamboat monopoly granted by NY state to an influential politician. After the victory, Thomas Gibbons hired the young Vanderbilt to captain one of his steamboats. However, Vanderbilt continued to run his own shipping business on the side while he worked for Gibbons.

Thomas Gibbons became Vanderbilt's mentor. Vanderbilt watched as Gibbons used the profits from one part of his steamboat empire to undercut his competitor's prices in another part, ultimately forcing his competitors out of business. Under the tutelage of Gibbons, Vanderbilt learned to operate a large and complicated business.

After Gibbons's death, Vanderbilt used the lessons he had learned from Gibbons to expand his own shipping empire. Vanderbilt also observed how President Andrew Jackson used populist language to gain support for his various programs. Vanderbilt took the lessons he learned from Gibbons and combined them with President Jackson's lessons. In addition to undercutting the fares of his competitors on the Hudson River, Vanderbilt named his line "The People's Line" to gain popular support for his business. With popular support for his business and lower prices than his competitors, Vanderbilt left his competition with only one option if they wanted to stay in business. They had to pay Vanderbilt to stop competing with them.

Vanderbilt soon dominated the local shipping industry in and around NY. He expanded his empire to include ocean going steamships to ferry gold from the California Gold Rush from Panama to the East Coast. Even as he expanded his empire, Vanderbilt continued to employ Gibbons's lessons about undercutting the competition until they either paid him to not compete or they went bankrupt and he took over their company.

With the emerging Industrial Revolution, Vanderbilt saw that the railroad business was the future and would soon replace much of the ferry business.

He began a campaign to take over the Stonington Railroad, a most attractive asset. He started by buying up some of the smaller connecting railroad lines and cutting fares, a trick he learned from his steamboat enterprise.

When he owned the choke points, he blocked the Stonington Railroad from having access to New York City. Fearing bankruptcy, Stonington Railroad 's stockholders started to sell their stock. When the stock price hit rock bottom, Vanderbilt was able buy their stock at an incredibly low price and take over.

With control of the Stonington Railroad, Vanderbilt decided to sell all of his ships so he could concentrate on the railroad industry. He connected several of his railroads and built Grand Central Station in the heart of New York City.

After a dispute with the treasurer of the Erie Railroad, Vanderbilt plotted revenge and set his sights on connecting his railroads to Chicago by acquiring the Erie Railroad in a hostile takeover. However, Jay Gould and Jim Fisk, the financiers of the Erie Railroad, spotted Vanderbilt's plot and began illegally printing new stock in order to dilute it.

Since state law restricted the number of shares a company could issue, Gould and Fisk bribed local legislators to legalize the new stock. Unaware he was being played, Vanderbilt continued to buy up stock and was milked out of 7 million dollars, the equivalent of over 1 billion dollars in today's money.

Gould and Fisk bragged about what they did and Vanderbilt threatened a lawsuit. The legislators and the illegal act of printing stock certificates was exposed, allowing Vanderbilt to recover most of his money.

Always looking for an edge, Vanderbilt saw that oil was discovered in Pennsylvania and Ohio. He realized that Kerosine, the oil used to light lamps, would soon change the world by turning night into day. Vanderbilt reached out to a small oil company run by a 27 year old man named JD Rockefeller to make him a deal.

Vanderbilt agreed to give Rockefeller a steep discount on his Kerosine shipping costs if Rockefeller shipped 60 train loads of Kerosine oil per day. Rockefeller agreed to this deal even though his Kerosine production at the time was only about half of the contracted amount.

Rockefeller agreed to Vanderbilt's terms because transportation costs were a large part of the price of retail Kerosine and this deal allowed Rockefeller to make his Kerosine much cheaper to his consumers, thereby increasing his business.

Cornelius Vanderbilt saw that the industry was changing from ferrying freight via water to moving freight via the railroad and was not afraid to change focus as the shipping industry evolved. Moreover, Vanderbilt took the lessons he learned from the steamboat industry and applied them to his railroad industry.

Vanderbilt also knew that pricing was the most powerful marketing tool a business owner could use to drive business.

Here are some lessons for the entrepreneur:

- Cornelius Vanderbilt became one of the captains of industry with little formal education.
- He found a mentor in Thomas Gibbons and took the lessons he learned to heart.
- He operated one business while employed in another.
- He learned that legislators could either create roadblocks or be used to clear them.
- He learned that if you had access to capital, you could subsidize portions of your business to drive out the competition or force them to pay you not to compete.
- He took a risk by partnering with a young entrepreneur in a rising industry.
- He understood that technology may cause you to pivot to capitalize on changing trends.

What lessons from Cornelius Vanderbilt's steamboat and railroad empires can you apply to your business?

Lessons from the Oil Magnate JD Rockefeller

JD Rockefeller grew up poor. His father, an unreliable con-man, sold snake oil to unsuspecting consumers. Although absent for most of JD's life, he instilled in Rockefeller an entrepreneurial spirit and mindset.

Rather than do chores like other kids his age, the young Rockefeller would buy a block of candy and cut it into small chunks to sell it to the neighborhood kids for a profit.

Being the eldest boy with an absentee father, he was forced to quit school to support the family. In addition to his candy enterprise, he also raised turkeys and sold potatoes. At one point, his own father cheated young Rockefeller. His father justified his actions by saying that he wanted to make JD sharp and teach him to always get the better part of a deal.

After his family moved from New York to Ohio, JD Rockefeller studied bookkeeping since he had an aptitude for numbers. At age 16, he got his first job as a bookkeeper and learned the inner workings of business. One day on his way home, he saw a wildcatter strike oil in Ohio and realized that oil would change world.

Rockefeller could see that drilling for oil was very risky

and not a very efficient way to make a living. After contemplating how to minimize his risks and capitalize on what he knew would be an up-and-coming oil boom, Rockefeller concluded that refining oil was safer and more profitable than drilling for it in the long run.

Having no background in oil, he found scientists to figure out how to refine oil into its usable components. In those early days, the principle product produced from crude oil was Kerosine, the oil used in lamps. Unfortunately not much was known about the refining process at that time and the products produced were inconsistent, resulting in some volatile varieties of Kerosine. In fact, Kerosine developed a negative reputation since some blends were highly combustible and could start fires.

By following the advice of his scientists, Rockefeller made a more consistent and less volatile product. Moreover, JD Rockefeller named his company "Standard Oil" because he knew that the name would show people that all Kerosine products with his brand name were uniform.

When the Civil War ended and the Great Westward Expansion began, a new oil-fueled economy was ushered in. By employing expert scientists, borrowing heavily, reinvesting his profits, and using his financial acumen to manage his costs, Rockefeller was able to be more efficient than his competitors.

He leveraged his position in the quickly expanding industry

and soon Standard Oil was the most profitable refiner in Ohio.

The railroads were fighting among themselves to control his freight traffic. Rockefeller was contacted by Cornelius Vanderbilt. Vanderbilt offered Standard Oil steep discounts over standard shipping costs provided that Standard Oil could ship 60 train loads of Kerosine per day. Rockefeller agreed to the deal even though his production volume at the time was less then half the contracted amount. However, he knew that a deal with Vanderbilt would increase his profit margins and thereby grab the attention of investors. He was right. Investors came on board to meet and exceed Vanderbilt's demand.

With Standard Oil stock on the rise, Rockefeller started to buy out his competitors. In a 4 month span, Standard Oil absorbed 22 of Cleveland's 26 refineries and Rockefeller was swimming in product.

A rival railroad to Vanderbilt's was the Pennsylvania Railroad. Tom Scott, vice president and financier of the Pennsylvania Railroad, took notice of Standard Oil's rapid expansion. Scott had an idea to create a cartel between the railroad and oil to control prices. The Pennsylvania Railroad offered Standard Oil a better deal than Vanderbilt to be part of their cartel by transporting his Kerosine on their rail lines. Rather than break the deal with Vanderbilt, Rockefeller played the railroads against each other to attempt to get an even better deal. However, this move backfired as Scott and Vanderbilt felt Rockefeller was angling for too much control and they colluded to marginalize Rockefeller.

Using a tactic Vanderbilt used to build his empire, Scott and Vanderbilt agreed that neither company would offer Rockefeller a discounted rate and charged him triple what he was previously paying in the hopes of bankrupting Standard Oil. Rockefeller saw this action for what is was: an act of war.

Appearing to be at the mercy of Vanderbilt and Scott, Rockefeller looked for a way to strengthen his position. A solution to JD Rockefeller's dilemma came from an unlikely place. To transport oil from its source at the well to either a railroad terminal or local refinery, teamsters charged exorbitant rates since the oil producer's options were limited. In fact, the transportation cost charged by the teamsters to transfer a barrel of crude oil by horse only a few miles to a railroad station or nearby refinery exceeded the cost of shipping a similar barrel of Kerosine by rail from Cleveland all the way to the East Coast.

In response, some oil producers began to invest in pipelines to transfer their crude oil to a refinery, proving that oil could be transported by pipeline to bypass the teamsters. Rockefeller figured that if a pipeline could transfer oil from the oil well to a refinery, a huge network of pipelines could link wells to refineries, cutting out both the teamsters and the railroads all together from the lucrative oil shipping business.

Although building a pipeline of this scale was a massive investment and came with significant risks, Rockefeller was driven to win in his feud with the railroads at all costs.

When the pipeline was complete, it was 4,000 miles in length and connected wells in Ohio, Pennsylvania, and West Virginia to his refineries in Cleveland. The pipeline was a huge blow to many area railroads since 40% of the cargo shipped by the railroads was from Standard Oil.

Rockefeller's pipeline exposed the fact that the railroad industry was over built and relied too heavily on a single customer, Standard Oil. Many small railroad companies went bankrupt and stock prices fell, busting the railroad bubble. One third of railroads went bankrupt in the resulting 1873 crash.

As Vanderbilt had done before, Rockefeller saw this as opportunity to build his own distribution system. Standard Oil agreed to sign contracts with strategic railroads that were failing to keep them afloat. However, in gratitude for his business, the railroad would have to agree to "drawbacks," which were essentially rebates offered to Standard Oil for shipments made by his competitors.

All he needed to do was show them their books, so they knew what they was up against, and make them a decent offer. If the railroad declined, Rockefeller would run them into bankruptcy and buy up their business at a fire sale when the bottom fell out of their stock.

He would then use the newly acquired railroad to expand his own distribution system. The Pennsylvania Railroad operated by Scott was outside Rockefeller's pipeline control so Standard Oil was still forced to use their railroad to ship his product to market.

Since two thirds of the Pennsylvania Railroad's oil freight was from Standard Oil, they knew it was only a matter of time before Rockefeller would be gunning for them too. Scott's plan was to diversify so he built his own pipelines and decided to get into the lucrative oil business himself.

When Rockefeller became aware of Scott's plan, he offered Scott an ultimatum – Quit the oil business or Standard Oil would pull all of its shipments from the Pennsylvania Railroad. Scott knew that his Pennsylvania Railroad was the only railroad between Pennsylvania and New York, a route Standard Oil needed to get Kerosine from its refinery in Pittsburgh to customers in New York.

Just as when he partnered with Vanderbilt, Scott felt that he had leverage over Rockefeller and said "no deal." Based on Scott's reply, Rockefeller pulled his shipments from the Pennsylvania Railroad and shut down his Pittsburgh refinery as threatened.

While this move hurt Standard Oil, Rockefeller knew it

would hurt Scott's Pennsylvania Railroad far more. In fact, Scott was forced to lay off half of his workers. In response to the massive layoff, workers at the Pennsylvania Railroad rioted and burnt down 39 buildings and destroyed 1200 train cars. By the end of the day, the Pennsylvania Railroad was in ruins.

With the advent of electricity, Rockefeller saw that the demand for Kerosine would soon wain as the principle source of light in people's homes. Like any good entrepreneur, he looked for a solution to his problem.

Originally, gasoline was the fuel component that was factored out of crude oil to make the more stable Kerosine product. Gasoline was considered a waste byproduct that was disposed of. Convinced that there must be a use for the highly flammable gasoline, he hired a team of scientists to see if there was a practical use for it.

The developers of the internal combustion engine were looking for fuel and Rockefeller had the answer in gasoline. Rockefeller began to buy internal combustion engines and use the gasoline byproduct of his refinery to power the refinery's own machines.

The timing was perfect as engineers were incorporating the internal combustion engines into carriages. Thus the automobile industry was born, fueling the next wave of growth for Standard Oil and making JD Rockefeller the world's first billionaire.

Here are some lessons for the entrepreneur:

- Rockefeller created a near monopoly with Standard Oil, controlling 90% of the US oil supply by the time Rockefeller was just 33 years old.
- He owed much of his success to a focused education in finance and knowing how to keep his costs down.
- He knew the value of community and surrounded himself with competent experts.
- He used leverage in the form of debt and equity investments to make the most of situations.
- Rockefeller knew enough to change course when the market was against him.
- He knew that wherever there is uncertainty, there is also opportunity.
- He treated business like a game, a game to win.
- He always looked for leap frog technology and was never complacent.
- He found solutions to problems by looking to other industries.
- He always looked for the checkmate move.
- He also remained semi-paranoid about what his competitors were doing.
- He knew that you make money by buying when the market and competition is down.
- Finally, the greed of the teamsters and the railroad caused their customers to find workarounds and cut

them out of the business altogether.

What lessons from the history of JD Rockefeller and Standard Oil can you apply to your business?

Lessons from the Steel Baron Andrew Carnegie

Andrew Carnegie grew up poor like JD Rockefeller and was forced to go to work at age 13 to support his family.

Although Carnegie had little formal schooling, he was very bright. When he was 15, he got a job as a telegraph messenger. By 18, he got a job as a telegraph operator with the Pennsylvania Railroad and met Thomas Scott who took the young Carnegie under his wing. The confidence that Scott showed in Carnegie bred confidence in Carnegie himself.

The Mississippi River represented a barrier for the railroads. Since the Mississippi River was so wide and large steamships used it to move freight up and down the river. Rail freight traveling across the country had to be unloaded on one side, ferried across the river on ships, and reloaded on rail cars on the other side to continue their journey.

Scott tasked Carnegie to build a railroad bridge across the Mississippi River at St. Louis. A railroad bridge across the central portion of the Mississippi River would open up the west to rail freight and represent huge profits for the railroad that could construct it.

The task represented the biggest bridge construction effort ever contemplated. It would require a span of over 1 mile in length and would have to be high enough to allow steamboat traffic to pass underneath it.

Carnegie bet the farm that he could do it. All bridges up to that point were made of either wood or stone, neither of which would work given the unsupported distances involved to allow steamships to pass. Iron was the metal of the day, but was not strong enough either. Yet steel, which mixes iron with carbon, was strong enough but very expensive.

To make a single steel rail took 2 weeks. However, in the summer of 1872, Carnegie learned of a scientist in England by the name of Henry Besimmer who had devised a technology that could produce a steel rail in just 15 minutes.

At 33 years old, Andrew Carnegie was poised to build the first bridge across the Mississippi River using steel. However, using steel delayed the project by two years and the project was flooded in debt. When the project's funds were exhausted, bridge construction was forced to stop.

The difference between those that succeed and those that fail is what they do when faced with adversity. Carnegie believe in the project and was all in personally. He would not give up and continued to search for investors. His perseverance finally paid off and he was able to secure the additional funding to complete the bridge.

On a summer day in 1874, the bridge was completed. However, people unfamiliar with the strength of steel feared that the bridge would collapse. Ever the showman, Andrew Carnegie employed an elephant to lead a procession of individuals across the bridge.

Knowing that steel would revolutionize the construction industry, Carnegie went to his mentor Thomas Scott to help him raise the capital needed to build his own steel plant.

His steel plant would be based on the blast furnace technology invented by Henry Besimmer in England. As the plant was being built, the 1873 crash hit and crippled the railroad industry. When the plant was competed 2 years later in 1875, Carnegie needed to make sure he had the customers to buy his steel, so he named the plant after Edger Thompson, Thomas Scott's partner and president of the Pennsylvania Railroad. By doing so, he won a huge contract to produce steel rails for the Pennsylvania Railroad.

A few years later, his life long mentor Thomas Scott died and Carnegie blamed JD Rockefeller for the death of his mentor and for the 1873 crash that hurt his biggest customers, the railroads.

However, there was an unexpected consequence to the crash. With the crash, people flooded into the cities looking for food and work. With demand for railroad steel waning, Carnegie saw an opportunity to provide structural steel to build high rise buildings. Soon steel became the single major component that made the construction of skyscrapers possible.

Carnegie was motivated by revenge for his friend Thomas Scott's death and vowed to surpass the wealth of JD Rockefeller which he knew was important to Rockefeller. Carnegie hired Henry Frick, a former coal baron who was merciless in his business dealings. The personalities of Carnegie and Frick were polar opposites. Carnegie didn't have the stomach to be a ruthless business man, but Flick did.

As a first mover, Carnegie Steel had the ability to press their advantage and Frick was the man to make that happen. Through the use of intimidation and fear, Frick was able buy out their competitors and grow Carnegie Steel, which pleased Andrew Carnegie. Carnegie promoted Frick to chairman of Carnegie Steel, but Frick had his eye on a bigger prize: Carnegie's job.

To gather support from rich and powerful partners to assist him on his quest to oust Carnegie, Henry Frick created an exclusive men's club for the rich and famous. This club was on a lake created by the South Fork dam upstream of Johnstown PA. Engineers told Frick that the dam needed to be strengthened, but Frick was in a hurry to gain influence and ignored the pleas of the engineers and the residents of

Johnstown. Moreover Frick wanted the road on top of the dam widened so motorists could travel across it. However, the only way to do that was to lower the dam which they did.

On Memorial Day 1889, it began to rain. The water level in the lake rose by 1 inch every 10 minutes and a dam breach looked imminent. Even though a warning was sent to the residents of Johnstown, most simple ignored it as they had seen other storms raise the water level with no consequences. Yet that was before the top of the dam was lowered to accommodate Frick's new road.

The dam broke, sending a torrent of water down the valley toward Johnstown. Over 2,000 people were killed and it was the worst man made disaster until 9/11. While Carnegie was a member of the club, it was Frick's actions that created the situation. The event however forever changed Andrew Carnegie since he felt responsible and his brand was forever tarnished.

Andrew Carnegie donated millions of dollars to rebuild Johnstown. He wanted to be remembered for the good he had done. He began to give away his money to build libraries and his crown jewel, Carnegie Hall, in New York City.

Carnegie renewed his rivalry with Rockefeller and knew he needed profits to become richer than Rockefeller. He built new steel plants and to keep cost down, he cut each worker's pay and demanded that they work longer hours.

He turned again to Frick to do his dirty work and left for Europe as he was prone to do to think and take stock of the industry away from the day to day operations. Frick instituted 12 hour days and 6 days a week work schedules.

There were no labor laws at the time so a group of workers decided to raise their concerns and organized a labor union. In June 1892, a worker died in an industrial accident at a steel plant, which galvanizes the other workers. Frick proclaimed that Carnegie Steel did not recognize the union and said that Carnegie Steel would not negotiate with its workforce. A strike ensued. Two thousand workers barricaded themselves inside the front gates to avoid scabs from replacing them.

Undaunted, Frick called in the Pinkertons, which was essentially a group of hired guns to break up the strike. Frick thought the sight of the armed Pinkertons would make the workers come to their senses and give up the strike. The workers stood their ground. Events continued to unfold and 9 workers were killed. Countless others were injured, but the workers continued to hold their ground.

The governor of Pennsylvania was forced to send in the state militia to restore order. Frick was held personally responsible for the killing and maiming of the workers by the employees of Carnegie Steel. An attempt was made by one of the workers to kill him.

Hearing the news of the killings, Carnegie returned from Europe and his relationship with Frick reached a breaking point. Frick told Carnegie that he should be head of Carnegie Steel since he did all the dirty work and even took a bullet for this effort. In public, each blamed the other for the misfortunes that were befalling Carnegie Steel.

At this point, JP Morgan entered the scene. JP Morgan was a financier who bought up failing businesses and returned them to profitability through consolidation. With all the issues facing Carnegie Steel, Carnegie was sure that Carnegie Steel was JP Morgan's next target. To avoid this misfortune, Carnegie decided to make a bold move and removed Henry Frick. With Frick out of the picture, Andrew Carnegie vowed to return Carnegie Steel to it's former greatness.

As was the case with RD Rockefeller and the advent of the internal combustion engine that breathed new life into Standard Oil, the Navy recognized the value of steel and submitted orders for steel warships to be constructed by Carnegie Steel. This made Carnegie Steel one of the first defense contractors and breathed new life into Carnegie's empire when he needed it most. The Navy contracts averted a power struggle with JP Morgan, at least for the time being.

Here are some lessons for the entrepreneur:
- Andrew Carnegie was always looking for the opportunity to advance his knowledge and rose

quickly in the Pennsylvania Railroad. By having a mentor, he learned the business.

- He kept abreast of technical events even when their applications were not obvious.
- He found solutions to problems by looking to other industries.
- He took risks and went all in so there was no turning back.
- He never gave up even when it looked like he would be unable to compete the project due to a lack of funds.
- He understood that sometimes you have to use showmanship to show people you are are right.
- He knew that you needed partners that complement your skills and hired Frick, his polar opposite, to fill that gap. The lesson is to not hire a weaker version of yourself, but to hire people that shore up your weaknesses. Carnegie's character would not allow him to be the villain so he hired one in Frick.
- Sometimes you need a rival, as he had with JD Rockefeller, to provide the personal drive needed to remain aggressive.
- Being a little paranoid about your competition, as he was with JP Morgan, can keep you focused and expose new opportunities.
- Finally, as the idea guy, Carnegie traveled for about 6 months out of the year to expose himself to new ideas and think on how he might apply these lessons in the steel business.

What lessons from Andrew Carnegie can you apply to your business?

Lessons from the International Financier JP Morgan

JP Morgan benefited from the best education money could buy. His father was a international banker, but he had a strained relationship with his son throughout his life. After high school, his father sent him to the best schools in France and Germany before setting his son up in his banking empire.

JP Morgan learned at a young age that to make money you had to invest other people's money. As the head of the most powerful banking house of the world, JP Morgan was focused on the reorganization and consolidation of distressed businesses.

When the financially troubled railroads fell on hard times after the crash of 1873, JP Morgan bought many of them, consolidated them, and reorganized their business structures and management in order to return them to profitability. He became so proficient at it that the the process of taking over troubled businesses to reorganize them became known as "Morganization."

His reputation as a banker and financier also helped bring interest from investors to the businesses he took over.

However, he became restless and when he turned 40, he felt

the need to get out from under his father. He saw what JD Rockefeller and Andrew Carnegie had done building their companies from the ground up and he wanted to do the same even though it was against his father's wishes.

Morgan knew it would take innovation and he took notice of an inventor named Thomas Edison. He wanted to invest in Edison's electric light business because he saw the potential of the electric light. To attract other investors, he had Edison install 400 electric lights in his New York home on 5th Avenue. He invited many of his wealthy friends to visit his home to demonstrate the electric light. JP Morgan's father disapproved, but the event was a success.

The demonstration made JD Rockefeller take stock in his own business as the Kerosine his company was built upon would soon be eclipsed by the electric light bulb. JP Morgan made the decision to fund Edison's idea and built a power grid to electrify half of New York City. Every home electrified by Edison was a lost customer for Rockefeller.

In an effort to protect his Kerosine empire, Rockefeller launched a media campaign to discredit electricity.

Edison's electricity transmission was based in Direct Current (DC), which anyone that has installed a car stereo amplifier knows that to transmit DC power without significant transmission loss requires the use of expensive heavy copper wires. Nicola Tesla, Edison's apprentice had discovered Alternating Current (AC), which overcame the transmission issues associated with DC. Tesla tried to influence Thomas Edison's thinking and encourage him to switch to AC. However, Edison's ego kept him from seeing the value of AC and he continued to focus on DC as the source of power for his electric light.

Both Edison and Tesla were idea people, but terrible business people. Frustrated by Edison's lack of recognition for his ideas, Tesla finally accepted an offer from George Westinghouse, an inventor and engineer in his own right, to invest in Tesla's AC idea. This set up what was known as the "Current War."

JP Morgan put the pressure on Edison to discredit AC and protect his investment. Edison agreed to set up demonstrations using AC to electrocute animals to show people that AC is an unsafe way to transmit electricity. After this demonstration, prisons looking for a more humane way of killing death row inmates contacted Edison. Edison saw this as a great demonstration to discredit AC and devised an electric chair using a Westinghouse generator and alternating current.

The first execution by electrocution took eight minutes and essentially roasted the man alive. People were horrified by the display and the stunt backfired on Edison who was forever associated with it.

JP Morgan's father ordered JP to divest himself of the electric industry, but JP hesitated, knowing that a large power plant in Niagara Falls was being built. However, it was not clear if the contract would be awarded to AC or DC power.

As he tried to make the decision to either defy his father or not, his father died in an accident and JP inherited his father's vast portfolio of investments. To hedge his bet of winning the Niagara Falls contract, he organized a smear campaign to trigger a sell-off of Westinghouse stock when Westinghouse was drowning in debt. The smear campaign left Westinghouse on the verge of ruin and unable to raise new money.

JP Morgan was convinced his plan had worked and that Westinghouse was out of the picture and he would be a shoe-in to get the Niagara Fall power plant contract. In a turn of fate, Tesla volunteered to void his royalty agreements with Westinghouse, giving George full control of the AC invention and with it the power to raise new money.

In a show of power, Westinghouse under bid JP Morgan to light the upcoming World's Fair in Chicago with AC lights at 1/4 the price of Morgan. Westinghouse won the bid easily. When they flipped the switch at the Chicago World's Fair, 200,000 lights came to life in a spectacular display. The world saw the power of AC and the Niagara Falls power plant contract was awarded to Westinghouse.

Even though Morgan and Edison lost the bid, JP Morgan

saw a way out. He told Westinghouse he would sue for patent infringement since Nicola Tesla was working at Edison Light when he discovered AC technology. With the huge financial resources at Morgan's disposal, Westinghouse had no other option but to hand over the patents to Morgan. Morgan then bought up all the shares in Edison General Electric to marginalize Thomas Edison and renamed the company General Electric (GE).

With Edison out of the way and the AC patents in hand, JP Morgan realized his dream of owning the electric industry and built GE into a powerhouse.

A lesson from the early history of JP Morgan is that you can make money by using other peoples money to leverage your own equity stake. You make money when you buy not when you sell. Troubled businesses and businesses in fierce head-to-head competition make easy targets for acquisition for some one with money. And finally sometimes you need a make a grand display to win hearts and minds as Morgan did by electrifying his home. What lessons from JP Morgan can you apply to your business?

Here are some lessons for the entrepreneur:
- One of the lesson from the JP Morgan story is that most inventors like Edison and Tesla, are not the best business people. They are less interesting in making money and more interest in being recognized of their idea and getting out in the public domain. It took JP Morgan to bring the light bulb

out from the lab and into commercialization. It took Westinghouse to make Tesla's AC see the light of day.

- Another lesson is that sometimes you need a make a grand display to win hearts and minds as Morgan did by electrifying his home and how Westinghouse did with the Chicago World's Fair.
- It is never a good idea to take your eye off the ball as Morgan did when he thought he had Westinghouse on the ropes.
- Also in business, you have to understand who you need to massage, who to knock in the head, and who you need to buy off to consolidate power. That is the game of business and it was the game JP Morgan did with the stock market, railroads, and electric industry.

What lessons from JP Morgan can you apply to your business?

How to Stop the American Industrial Revolution

JP Morgan was known for locating companies that were fighting each other and who were in financial trouble. He would then bring them these companies together and manage them in such a way that competition was reduced and inefficiencies could be eliminated.

Through consolidation, he would merge and eliminate jobs to improve the company's value by increasing profits over everything else. Soon his rivals Andrew Carnegie and JD Rockefeller saw his wisdom and followed suit. They cut workers and forced the ones with jobs to work harder for less pay. The gap between rich and poor grew and the captains of the Industrial Revolution were soon depicted as the symbols of everything that was wrong with America.

Williams Jennings Bryant was a politician running for President of the United States. His platform offered hope and change to the middle class. He vowed to put an end to the monopolies. Since public opinion was solidly against the remaining captains of industry, Rockefeller, Carnegie, and Morgan agreed to put their rivalries aside and work together.

Since Bryant was running for President, they figured their best plan of attack was to use their wealth to buy political favor with the President of the United States. They made the decision to back William McKinley's presidential run against Bryant and funded McKinley's campaign.

They used their influence as major employers by telling their employees that if Bryant won the election on Tuesday, don't bother to show up for work on Wednesday as they would be shutting down. This fear tactic caused 90% of the population to vote. There was no secret ballot back then and everyone knew who you voted for. There was a line to cast your vote for the the Republican McKinley and a line for the Democrat Bryant. Supervisors could observed who you voted for. McKinley won the election, making all of the issues not favorable to captains of industry disappear.

With the election behind them, it was back to business as usual. JD Rockefeller renewed his rivalry with Carnegie and blocked Andrew Carnegie's expansion by buying up iron ore mines and selling the ore to Carnegie's competitors at rock bottom prices.

Carnegie Steel lost many of their customers to their competitors based on price. Then JD Rockefeller made plans to build steel plants to compete head to head with Carnegie. Andrew Carnegie agreed to buy all the ore from Rockefeller if he elected not to build competing steel plants. The agreement satisfied Rockefeller since his biggest rival, Andrew Carnegie, would be paying to make him even richer.

Seeing blood in the water, JP Morgan used his influence in mining and railroads to consolidate the steel industry. Andrew Carnegie, already hurting from his battle with Rockefeller, was in no condition to take on Morgan.

In a move, Morgan backed Charles Schwab, Carnegie Steel's new number two man in a deal to buy Carnegie Steel for $480 million. To put that offer into prospective, $480 million dollars in today's dollars is more than the entire federal budget, at that time, plus the net worth of Warren Buffet and Bill Gates fortunes combined.

Carnegie agreed to sell Carnegie Steel and became the richest man in history. In today's money, Carnegie was worth the equivalent of $310 billion dollars. The new company under Charles Schwab became known as "US Steel."

Andrew Carnegie's exit timing was perfect because in that same year William McKinley was assassinated and Theodore Roosevelt, the former Governor of New York and McKinley's VP, became President of the United States.

In a turn of fate, William McKinley was assassinated by a guy who lost his job when JP Morgan bought out Andrew Carnegie to create US Steel and felt that President McKinley was too close to big business.

For Morgan and Rockefeller, their worst nightmares emerged as Roosevelt became President because unlike

McKinley, they could not buy Roosevelt.

Historically, the Vice President of the United States was a powerless position and were non-entities in politics. Moreover, the VP was never destined to become President.

Roosevelt now President, was known for the fair deal and as a trust buster. The antitrust movement under Roosevelt broke up JP Morgan's railroad empire. JP Morgan used his influence however to keep US Steel out of Roosevelt's cross hairs by helping to broker a deal to build the Panama Canal, a pet project of Roosevelt.

Next up for Roosevelt was Rockefeller's Standard Oil. Standard Oil was broken up into 34 smaller companies. Some of those company's went on to become Exxon, Mobil, and Chevron. Rockefeller remained their largest stockholder and made even more money than before. Rockefeller's net worth amounted to $660 billion in today's money and he achieved his goal of becoming the richest man, surpassing his rival Andrew Carnegie.

In the final chapter, Henry Ford developed the people's car. Prior to Ford, all cars were chauffeur driven and were only for the ultra-rich. However, a monopoly owned the patent on all cars produced and they demanded a steep royalty on all of Ford's cars, making them much less affordable for the average man.

Henry Ford banked on the trend that monopolies were

being busted up and continued building his cars in spite of the patent law suit against Ford. Ford even agreed to pay his workers double the scale rate and became know as the anti-captain of industry who cared about the worker.

The court ruled that Ford's car was not covered by the patent and Ford rode the anti-monopoly wave into history. The cars that Ford produced were fueled by the gasoline that was made possible by Rockefeller's Standard Oil. The cars were made with the steel that was produced by Andrew Carnegie and built in a plant powered by JP Morgan's Electricity.

During an approximately 35 year period starting at the end of the Civil War until the turn of the century, the United States experienced one of its greatest periods of innovation: The American Industrial Revolution.

The American Industrial Revolution was made possible by men that risked everything time and time again, men who raised the standard of living for every American and created what we now call the middle class. These men launched the United States into an era of prosperity after the Civil War and helped to establish America as the richest nation in the world.

Andrew Carnegie gave away the equivalent of $67 billion to build libraries and JD Rockefeller created the Rockefeller Foundation, which gave away the equivalent of $38 billion to advance public health.

The captains of industry may have been ruthless business men and fierce competitors that used their power and money to control their competition, but they did so with their own money and improved the quality of life for all Americans.

Without the likes of JP Morgan, the man who used his power and influence to help save the nation by loaning the federal government more than $60 million and convinced the country's top financiers to bail out faltering financial institutions in order to stabilize the market, who knows where America would be today?

Not a bad track record for men who the federal government convinced Unites States citizens that these men were robber barons who deserved to be crushed so these same political leaders could advance their own careers.

The federal government has a history of squelching the successful entrepreneur by spinning a story for its own political gain. The Sherman Antitrust Act of 1890 was used to break up Standard Oil and Morgan's railroads. It was used more recently to break up AT&T and force Microsoft to give away its propitiatory API to third party companies.

How has the idea of a successful businesses led by competent leaders been spun into something bad that the government feels they need to protect us all against?

What lessons from the stories of the captains of the American Industrial Revolution can you apply to your business?

Moreover, what can you do to keep the federal government from killing the spirit of the American businessman?

Chapter 3: Bonus Business Lessons

Sometimes businesses and not specifically their founders and CEOs can change the trajectory of markets. As a bonus here are a few lessons from businesses that changed their business and economic models and as such contain some valuable lessons for the entrepreneur.

New Economic Model Propels Xerox

Many local ecosystems have initiatives and programs to foster innovation in their own community as a way to grow new technology or manufacturing companies. They do this in the hopes it will bring in new money as the primary employer grows to maturity. However, sometimes it is not the product that generates the revenue, but a new economic model that makes a business viable and become a primary employer.

Take for instance the case of Chester Carlson. He invented the process of electrophotography which is known as photocopying today. However, the copier technology was not sufficient to be marketable. In fact, Chester attempted to make electrophotography a viable business, but met with a long history of failures.

John Dessauer, Chief of Research at the Haloid Company of Rochester NY, read an article about Carlson's invention and licensed the technology. Haloid was a manufacturer of photographic paper and was looking for a way to reinvent itself. Haloid changed its company name to Xerox and went on to produce the first commercial photocopier known as the XeroX Model A. He also later produced the first plain paper copier known simply as the 914.

However, because photocopy machines were very expensive, sales remained poor. In the end, neither the technology or the manufacturing capability produced much economic value. The photocopier did not take off until they changed the economic model from selling the copiers to leasing them and paying for copies.

Licensing the technology and changing the economic model made Xerox a viable company. As the Xerox story illustrates, it may not be the product inventor or the product producer that may capture value, but the person that has a new economic model to capture value in a new way. All it may take is a keen mind to come up with a new economic model to capture the real value.

Can you change your economic model to capture a greater share of your market?

New Business Model Propels Keurig

Fifty percent of Americans over 18 years of age drink coffee every day. That translates into 150 million daily coffee drinkers that consume 400 million cups per day.

Not long ago, brewing a cup of coffee at home or at the office involved purchasing a coffee pot from one company and ground coffee from another company. Then, you had to make the coffee a whole pot at a time.

Enter Keurig with a new business model for single serve coffee. Originally, Keurig focused on selling the single serve coffee machines to businesses as an alternative to the more traditional coffee pot system. The business model was a failure since the cost of the machine was too high.

Keurig knew it was time for a pivot and began to look at the home market. However, before it could become a viable alternative in the home market, he had to figure out a way to get Americans to throw away their existing coffee pots and buy into the new Keurig single cup system.

First off, Keurig made the decision that profits would not be made on the machine, but on the K-cups. They subcontracted the manufacture of the machines and tacked on no margin to keep the wholesale price of the machine cheap.

Since the wholesale price that retailers paid of the machine was low, retailers could mark them up and capture a higher margin on Keurig machines. Retailers loved it and were eager to sell more of the Keurig coffee machines to the public.

Once the consumer bought the machines, they were locked into the Keurig pods. Keurig developed his own Business to Consumer (B2C) distribution channel and sold the K-cups directly to consumers so they could capture the full margin instead of adopting a Business to Business (B2B) model of shipping pallets of K-cups to retailers. In this way, Keurig could capture a larger reoccurring retail sale price margin rather than having to settle for the much smaller wholesale price margin.

While the Keurig business and economic model has evolved, the lesson for the entrepreneur is to challenge existing business and economic models to extract value.

When was the last time you looked at your business with a critical eye to see if changing your business or economic model could propel your business to the next level?

Zappos Learns Demand

A fellow mentor who is an expert in retail once shared with me that opening a shoe store is one of the most risky businesses to start and operate because there are so many bad assumptions you can make.

In a typical main street brick and mortar shoe store, you have to select and stock the proper proportions of style, size, and color. Getting only two of the three right could sink your business hopes.

A few months back, I took my mom shopping for a new pair of comfortable, everyday, walking shoes. After looking at several styles and trying on several pairs of shoes, she found a pair she loved. They looked good and fit great, but after a check of the store's stock, it only came in a color she could not live with so there was no sale.

When starting out, Zappos, the online shoe retailer, faced the same problem and was not sure what products, sizes, or colors of shoes would sell. Rather than commit large amounts of capital on stock and gamble on selecting customer preferences correctly, Zappos founders went to local brick and mortar retailers and took pictures of their shoes and negotiated discount pricing. They then posted them on their newly developed website. Without the risk associated with the typical shoe store, Zappos was able to learn customer demand.

Dell computer dominated the personal computer market by not making assumptions about configurations their customers wanted, but by letting the customer build their own computer component by component.

Making bad assumptions about customer demands means that you have to steeply discount inventory, often for less than cost, that did not sell well. This negatively effects your margins and profits. Even if you can't get the best margins by making high volume purchases, your savings in not buying unwanted inventory often outweighs the lack of volume discounts and assumes less risk.

What strategies do you have in place to learn your customers' preferences?

Zappos Bribes New Employees to Quit

The online retailer Zappos is known for its top shelf customer service. One way Zappos excels at customer service is the amount of flexibility and discretion it gives its customer service representatives to make the customer happy.

Hiring and training the right customer service representative makes all the difference between success and failure at Zappos. Zappos puts new trainees through an extensive four week training program. At the one week point they make an unusual offer to their trainees. Each trainee is offered several thousand dollars to quit that day. Zappos figures that if a trainee can be lulled into quitting for a few thousand dollars they are not going to turn out to be the employee they want representing the company.

Zappos figures it is better to pay out a few thousand bucks after only a week than to continue the training process. Zappos does not want to get a person working with customers, only to learn that the employee is only there for the money and has no commitment or loyalty to the company.

How can you use the lesson from Zappos to test your employee's level of commitment?